Primate
Behavior

Primate
Behavior

Sarah Lindsay

Grove Press
New York

For Mom and Dad
who gave me books

Published simultaneously in Canada
Printed in the United States of America

Library of Congress Cataloging-in-Publication Data

Lindsay, Sarah, 1958–
Primate behavior / Sarah Lindsay.
p. cm. — (Grove Press poetry series)
ISBN 0-8021-3557-9 (pbk.)
I. Title.
PS3562.I51192P75   1997
811'.54—dc21   97-11821

The author wishes to thank George Bradley and Kay Ryan for their generous and perspicacious help.

Grateful acknowledgment is made to the following publications, in which these poems first appeared:

The Cream City Review: "Superman in Sunglasses"; *Georgia Review*: "So Were the Animals," "Whether or Not a Giraffe Lies Down to Sleep"; *The New Republic*: "Dinosaur to Dragon"; *New Virginia Review*: "Primate Behavior"; *The Paris Review*: "Lungfish Conquers Depression," "Neanderthal"; *The Plum Review*: "Musk Oxen Do Not Run Away"; *Poetry Motel*: "Of What Earth Has Eaten, Something May Yet Be Found"; *Prairie Schooner*: "Where Thieves Break In and Steal"; *Southwest Review*: "Alfred Russel Wallace in Venezuela"; *The Threepenny Review:* "Dido Summons the Beetles"; *The Yale Review*: "Aluminum Chlorohydrate"

DESIGN BY LAURA HAMMOND HOUGH

Grove Press
841 Broadway
New York, NY 10003

98 99 00 01   10 9 8 7 6 5 4 3 2

Contents

❦ I ❦

By Luristan to Thule 3

So Were the Animals 4

Constantinople, Plague Summer 6

The Angel That Troubled the Waters 7

Hidden at the Zoo 8

Nachtmusik 10

Voladora 11

Slumgullion 13

Superman in Sunglasses 15

US 16

Life on Earth, Part Twelve: The Business Salmon 17

Thor Swimming 18

Blue Oranges 20

Aluminum Chlorohydrate 21

What All It Takes 22

Tyrannosaurus Sex 24

Musk Oxen Do Not Run Away 25

Neanderthal 26

Lungfish Conquers Depression 27

Instead of Acceptance 28

Dinosaur to Dragon 29

They Live Here 30

Manatee in Honey 31

Honeysuckle 32

Honey 33

Legend of the Woolly Mammoth 34

Where Thieves Break In and Steal   36

Lassie's Left Eye   37

Accidentals   38

Chang and Eng View a Giraffe   39

Really Big Shew   40

Borodin: Symphony in B Minor   41

❧ II: Circus Merk ❦

Circus Merk at the End of the Flandrian Interglacial   45

Circus Merk's Queen of Siberia   46

See Circus Merk's Own Amazing Siamese Twins   48

Madame Vashti Sees the Future   49

Circus Merk and the Spectacular Conflagration   50

The Acts of the Elephants   51

The Hartunians Form the Tower in the Dark   52

Tornado Watch   54

Elephant Waltz   56

Professor Enjō's Astounding Continuum Ray   58

Circus Merk, 25,000 B.C.   60

Toby the Sapient Pig   61

The End of Circus Merk's Elephant Baseball Act   63

Dido Summons the Beetles   65

❧ III ❦

Capt. Robert Falcon Scott Returns to London   69

Warming: Aletsch Glacier   71

Whether or Not a Giraffe Lies Down to Sleep   72

Courthope on Pulau Run, 1620   74

Of What Earth Has Eaten, Something May Yet Be Found   76

Near Combe d'Arc   77

A Lizard, a Stone   78

Slides from Patagonia, 1896–99   80

Arsinoitherium   84

Solipsist in Love   85

Venus of Judith River   86

Positive White   87

Fossil Finds   88

His Hot Breath on Her Cheek   89

El Abuelo   90

The Wreck of the *General Grant*   92

Primate Behavior   94

Vegetables in Space   96

First Song for the *Ba* of Ptah-hotep   97

Buprestidae, Cantharidae   98

Alfred Russel Wallace in Venezuela   100

Cheese Penguin   102

I

By Luristan to Thule

Delirium was the last country she saw clearly.
Mounting its exotic, riven flanks
on the back of a patient fever,
she left with regret the land of her hosts—
divisions of snow, upended stone threaded with tracks
between the goatskin houses with goatskin beds—
then left too the regret.

For decades she'd taken pleasure in imposing
the first white profile (with its great spinster nose)
upon such places, barely named,
as lay a few days' journey beyond fable,
uplands that bore no showy gold or ziggurat,
only the shallow marks of laboring generations,
the central campfires repeated deep in their eyes.

Past rocks tipped early out of the cradle of myth,
she finally became separated from her pack
with its twenty pencils, the notorious hat,
coins and aspirin, equally useless,
and yielded to discovery of one state
that lacks the primary luxuries: return,
and the safely delivered story.

So Were the Animals

In that time,
before the sun wore red and yellow feathers,
before the sky's umbilicus parted,
the Machiguengas were people but so
were the animals, so were the plants,
so were the stars. Then Yabireri
breathed on this one and that
and made them toucans, cacao trees,
orchids, or giant otters.

Until Yabireri blew his breath
they were all people,
consuming granite, changing red light to sugar,
swallowing twelve-foot anacondas;
they were all people,
pushing each other's eggs from the nest,
streaming white fire that travels after they die,
changing from male to female;
they were all people,
weaving houses of grasses and bright blue trash,
folding dewlaps away and turning from orange to brown,
lapping blood from the small wounds of sleepers,
rolling themselves in balls, eating hot sulfur;
they were all people.

Two stopped the spirit god
before he could change them all.
There were still people
to drink ayahuasca and rise to the spirits,
to knit barbs in wire and string it wide,
to write down endless numbers,
to look into fire and sing till their eyes hurt
and still sing, to dam rivers,
to slit the belly of a thirteen-year-old girl,
to tear a mountain open and let it rust,

to trace an eyebrow with a wondering thumb,
to make stories out of everything.
There were still people
Yabireri could not blow out.
He watched from where they left him,
impaled on a wooden stake
at the mouth of the sky.

Constantinople, Plague Summer

Wind out of the north today, with the stench
from the towers across the Horn, where the emperor's men
have packed the dead. I danced for a man last night
with black peas all over his arms. When I placed my hands
on the floor, reaching over my head, he began to scream.
Spilled red fish sauce, I think, ran over the table.
I took all the food I could carry.

Those the plague passes over are starving.
I dreamt of ortolans in a pastry nest,
woke to another slave bolting to drown his fever.
They say plum pickle wards it off, or lemons;
they say God sends it. I think it's part of the world
that strikes and spares and never gives us the pattern.
Tertia, our best, went first.

They say the emperor prays all day.
Some say he is dying. He's sent for me, nonetheless.
No chin, like a rat, and his small hands are never still,
but if any wine is left in the city he'll have it,
olives and figs to push between my breasts,
perhaps little birds in a pie with fruit in their beaks
or spitted with their eyes open.

The Angel That Troubled the Waters

Who started this none of them can say,
not even those with tongues,
but families hear of the angel that troubles the waters
and deposit their last hopes beside the pool
in ragged rings.

And when the water ripples, what a surge
among the patients, hunched over their pain
in starting-line positions,
the broad-shouldered lame, the sniffing blind,
those clutching their bowels, their sores, their wild heads,
even the limbless ones—

but it's only a frog, or breeze, or a feather
fallen from great height.
They settle again, and continue to endure
belief in an angel who might hold such a race
and award but one prize.

A small mercy that it was a moonless night
when the angel of curiosity, meaning no harm,
stirred the pool with one long finger,
startled to taste
how salt it is, and warm.

Hidden at the Zoo

At first the keepers amused themselves,
pairing Mondrian with the zebras, El Greco with giraffes,
but as rumors of the enemy's approach
grew heads and teeth, sleepless curators
tried to run with straw-stuffed crates
and thrust their arms into dangerous cages
till half the museum was hidden at the zoo.

Throughout the occupation, the animals kept their secrets.
But their boredom was more stubborn
than a handful of hasty nails.
The elephant delicately picked straw
from the bust of Akhenaten;
the blue-cheeked mandrill bared its fangs
at the rival color patches of Rousseau.

Brown bears bedded down for the winter
in a cave lined with peaceable Rembrandts.
At night the slow loris watched
with its everlastingly startled eyes
as the aye-aye touched
its wire-thin long third finger
to a rosy Renoir chin.

In the reptile house a flying gecko
established that its purple-brown toes
adhered to Raphael's angels as to any wall,
and the Indian long-nosed tree snake
tested its rare binocular vision
and the whisper of its ventral scales
on the torso of an Apollonian youth.

As supplies ran short, one keeper discovered
he didn't mind his koalas gnawing
the frames of Renaissance triptychs. Another
covered his face and cursed his cowardly hands
as drunken soldiers played target practice,
as the white rhino knelt, taking the bullets
that could have pierced the Vermeer.

A month later the broken aviary emptied,
deserted by the orange minivet, the mandarin ducks,
the blue-backed fairy bluebird,
but the sociable weaverbirds stayed
at their communal tree, and threaded
the thatch of their nest with canvas strands
to which clung flecks of paint,

while next door in the butterfly house,
the ripening eggs of *Morpho,*
Papilio, Melanitis, and the rest prepared
to hatch their ravenous larvae.

Nachtmusik

Like him, she is old. Her neck curves like the violin's,
whose long harsh kiss shows on her jaw when she turns
to the tuning fork she's spanked on her knee,
her pursed lips drawing in the long thin *A*.

"Beethoven tonight? Mozart, Haydn? Brahms?"
she gloats absently over the sheets to his usual shrug;
he goes back to touching the cello strings with his thumbs.
She lifts her bow, and its hair falls loose from the frog

like a girl's. "Ach. It's always something, isn't it?
How we play such fragile things, I don't know,
they could fall apart in our hands." With her second bow
she tunes again. He doesn't see her rosin it;

bent over the cello's shoulder he has the sense
of remembering Berlin, the night a bomb
buried the bridegroom and all but one of his friends,
the night he knelt outside his gaping home

and heard the grand piano fall five floors—
heard its last five monstrous chords
that blotted out for years all the Bach he knew.
"Mozart, then," he says, and so they play.

Voladora

Naked and obedient in the moonless clearing
she rises on tiptoe, lifts her arms wide,
swallows her instructor's bitter syrup,
and vomits her entrails into the copper dish.
Loosed, lightened, with birdwings sprouting
so fast they hurt, she can barely stay
for the message of the invisible ones;
she carries it screaming high
through night air full of devils that brush her skin.

Mother, Mother— it is too late to pray
since she stood forty days forty nights half drowned
under Thraiguén waterfall and her true baptism
was plundered away and she begged for the bits
of toasted bread they held out on pointed sticks.
Most beautiful sister of a Brujería initiate
(who killed his best friend, who flayed the corpse
and made a vest of its skin that glows in the dark,
who passed other tests), she was chosen.
She begged them, the male witches.
Voladora, her brother whispers so no one else can hear,
Voladora, tonight. She walks to the forest.
Meets the dish. She flies screaming.

The Brujería, they change themselves to animals,
they enter men's dreams and drive them mad.
They alter the courses of rivers,
spread sickness that has no cure.
They injure whom they choose. *Voladora, tonight.*
She mounts the reeking velvet air,
lunges over the trees, unbalanced, high
where the weak lights scattered below can't see her.

Every secret message she bears
is a chain locked tight to her throat, a medallion
weight on her breast, red hot. Thirty years
she has done their bidding just so she can crouch
at dawn by the copper basin, furtively
wolf down her intestines,
and be human again, to the eye.

The poisonous night-moths fold away
and a bird speaks of dawn. She circles the place
where the bloody dish still shines. Is she hungry?
How long since she has been hungry?
What does she need with those innards, what need
for the form of that beautiful girl?
Let them look for her with the short-eared owl,
the carrion hawk, the mockingbird.
She flies silently. They will never get her back.

Slumgullion

The red-eyed pigeons disdain my suet
and chalky bread that once, as I remember,
enthralled them and all their cousins. "Rats with wings,"
sniffs the old lady around whose sensible shoes
they bowed smooth heads, in times gone by,
to a semicircle of peanuts. "Rats with wings."
Now exotic dinners are spread wherever they go:
clots in the streets, puddles and pockets
in the dirt, in the buckling grass,
of everything we let go, pass by, lose.

Three miners headed west to peck at any rich stain in the rocks.
(So say the brown letters one of them sent his grandson.)
Starving on the edge of a desert,
they found in a shallow cave some kind of molasses,
a chunky brittle secreted by stone. Like manna.
They ate till they were full at last,
and a little sick later. That candy was a pack-rat midden,
grass twigs leaves seeds cactus-spines and feathers,
bugs and pebbles, all ambered for the fossil record
with decades of pack-rat pee.

This is our nonelectronic diary now,
to go with the archives of car parts and mattress springs:
waste, all kinds, escaped and mingled in mats
becoming one mat, one flow of tepid lava.
Crumbs, tobacco, toothpaste, phlegm,
sticky half-inches in foam cups and reeking bottles,
sugar, ketchup, vials, diamonds,
unguents, tabloid drool, cough syrup, blood.
Unmentionable or unnoticed, in such volume
fat cockroaches can't keep up.

Rasped with stinking salt, the tongue
makes for itself a fugitive sweetness, like green
one sees after too much red. Stare at this dumping ground
long enough and angels appear in the sky.
But no one really minds his own smell,
or gnawing a bone if the spit on it is hers.
So sludge of gossip philosophy pudding and lint
lips at our ankles; later, when there are more of us,
we can mark its tides on our walls. And in the wilderness,
the fires of abandoned coal mines burning forty years
will be fed, or slaked at last.

Superman in Sunglasses

Little Clark, scuffing the toes of his Keds in the dirt,
lost in boredom wide as Nebraska, looked down.
Saw a pebble pinned under the arch of his foot,
saw earthworms tinily mouthing their way grain by grain,
tyrannosaur bones, articulate, spine strained back,
a seething fiery darkness of molten rock,
and the chipped red-painted sole of a Chinese clog.

Then the other sky. Wherever he looked after that for weeks
he saw space, the black outer space behind even the sun.
Needing to watch girls, he tried not to burn when he peeked
but saw past her underwear, past her secret skin
to viscera, ribs, and the writhing of her heart.
And saw a first egg begin its calm descent
before his steely focus came apart.

Later, with glasses, with practice by accident mostly,
he saw how his dried parents wanted him bound,
changing their tires forever, how compact Lois
was an angular mess of desire, and looking down
from Metropolis windows saw onion-skin slides stained
with lurid angers, gloating, love in vain,
the black familiar nodules in a villain's brain.

Now the curved lens's magnified rainbow reflection
shows him straggling eyebrow hairs, the step of the crow
on one side, the stare half an inch away
of his open blue-black blank eye.

US

This is not a country that needs me to speak for it

This is not a country with one great wound
        at which I can cry out
        and be heard

This is no place small enough for a cradle,
           no green palm of a hand, embraceable chain of red
           mountains

It will not condense, it will not yield to a single music,
        no two of its horizons take the same line

This is not a country that counts me
        when it goes to its storehouse to count,
        when it dials up majority wedges of pie,
        when it tunes in its screens with their Nielsen boxes

Not my mother, not my father,
        scatterer of sisters and brothers
        among the prairie-dog holes, the skyscraper ant farms

It's too big, too built to bury love in

The love spilled on it, viscous white, sticky red,
        won't soak in—scours the mere ground
        and bears it downhill

Dry rock lies by swollen rivers
        and the dry rocks groan
        and the rivers shout
        and sometimes they're on TV

This is not a country that asks me to speak

Life on Earth, Part Twelve:
The Business Salmon

When the season comes, unquestioningly
they abandon the ocean and thread themselves
through the mouths of their native rivers—
the males in their double-breasted suits,
their necktie stripes of steelhead, rainbow,
cutthroat, Dolly Varden, eastern brook;
the females in stern skirts and silky blouses.
Knees together, arms against their sides,
they swim against a current for the first time and the last,
convulsing up ladders, hurling themselves at rapids.
They forget to be tired, forget to eat.
The sunny, unsalt water flics apart on their padded shoulders.
By the time they reach the waters of their infancy,
their good leather shoes are scuffed, their briefcases battered,
buttons missing, hair undone. Sides heaving in and out.
Here the females deposit piles of paperwork
for the males to cover with blizzards of contracts and memos.
They are finished. In the quiet shallows they hover,
then lay their meager flesh on the riffled gravel.
Mouths wide open. Eyes wide open.
It does not look like rest. But they are
mostly washed away before
the children arise in thousands like snow falling upward
and career toward the sea in their little toboggan bodies,
without an idea in the world that deep in their brains some
    kink,
some microscopic hook, will make them want
to put on business clothes and swim upstream.

Thor Swimming

The polar bear comes to devour you.
Your destiny at last. You draw the door wide
open—he stands taller than the frame—
and fall back before him, *come in, come in,*
respectfully await his embrace.
I knew you would find me. I'm ready.
Surprisingly ready, even your gladness
stiff with expectation, as if with cold.
He will carry you, crushed and engulfed, north to the pack ice,
will hold you beneath his heart all the starving months,
his muscles sipping you just to keep moving—
the trace of you released through his nostrils
the only warmth to rise for aching miles around.

You've waited for him since you saw Thor swimming.
The Lincoln Park Zoo male in dead summer
took the false pool in his arms. Below
the surface on one side, a small blue window
showed him in oval, and how perfectly
he did not care that you watched
his mass in flight, a mountain bending,
a planet with blowing hair.
Of this movement, grace is an imitation.
Of his black eyes without depth
in the wedge of his face,
arrogance is a shadow.

You heard of his wicked ways:
baiting his cage with flung peanuts, pretending
sleep for hours till a duped squirrel
flickered near his paw and was struck by lightning.
Later, "napping" by the keeper's lost shoe.

On the ice where you will be going
there is no boredom, only expanse, and cold
too cold for smell. There are two kinds of taste:
the blade of the wind, and salt flesh
of anything that swims and is slow, which
the bear tastes no more than
he tastes his own tongue. There are
blue white and yellow white; nothing is dark
but what moves and is edible, or
what moves unbreathable under the ice.

The wonder before you, the throat cantilevered
in uncaressable fur. He drops to four paws
and opens his heavy mouth.
His teeth are brown stumps in a reek
of banana peel, rancid pork rind, battery acid.
The garbage bears of Churchill
live in the dump. They skip the nine-month fast,
rip open their stinking half-warm prey's
loose black plastic skin.
He shuffles around your spread hands to the couch
and, as you begin your miserable shiver,
drops. Sighs. Appears to watch TV.

Blue Oranges

One thousand miles inland from the original tree,
one in the box of leathery glowing globes begins
earlier than the others a web of brown lines on its skin.

Inside, the pale intricate membranes stretch and toughen.
They secretly drink the juice. The close-held seeds go dry.
The ball is less and less a ball, its flat spots sunken.

No more nourished or nourishing, the tender polyps
turn acid in their envelopes packed around the starry center,
decline from gorgeous orange to thin yellow, fermenting.

Superior fruits prefer to be removed from such
corruption, lest it prove contagious to the touch
despite its clear connection to some lack of moral fiber,

whereas the sagging browning merely overripe
may hate it simply, as the dim the blind,
consumingly, as the halt may hate the lame,

and in its powdery final rot and transmutation,
the closer the pale blue orange draws to its dusty cave-in
the more urgent its desire for something else to blame.

Aluminum Chlorohydrate

Am I then to understand
that with every matins' sociable embalming of the armpit
molecular aluminum insinuates itself, through sheared follicles,
bright fleck by bright invisible fleck, into the tiny tender kinks
of capillaries? slides along their permeable wisps
into the jostling rivers of depleted scarlet doughnuts and white
    ghosts,
into a hectic Amazon, through endlessly wrung chambers,
out the roaring wide aorta, rising blandly through the neck
by ever subtler pulses toward the tingling gray curd
all flushed with its matted electrical storms? and lays
a glinting finger on one sparked synaptic mouth
that hushes. Whose voice may never be missed.
A number, a name, the Latin for *greed*,
clopping upstairs that March day in Florence with brand-new
    clogs,
the blister they raised. But supposing senility
takes the brain in its soft retriever's mouth
and carries it to be gutted, supposing all
the recent layers plucked away and memory's microscopic
    doors flung wide
for the oldest to come forth: Would third-grade Ruth be missing
and unmissed, or Mary or Brenda, with random trivial
    comrades,
or would the whole host stagger out, one missing legs, another
    clothes,
with synthetic pearls for eyes or carrot noses?
Or would each corridor dead-end on a scaly tinfoil mirror
showing nothing but the scowling smear
of some old unfamiliar woman's face?

What All It Takes

Up and down its red and blue chutes
my defective blood bumps: Oreos and gumballs one hour,
famished soap bubbles the next. Christmas survived,
I find with the special sugarless candy's
mild laxative effect time to wonder
at what all it takes to keep me up.
The patches and stitches, the little glucose computer,
plastic packaging every day to the landfill,
and needles, a whole iron mine
could have run dry for me. The operations,
don't-touch bins all heaped with trays and
tubes and rubber gloves and miles of gauze.
Where it all comes from. The truckers, line workers,
underprivileged South American harvesters,
and patent holders that put together
one lousy just-in-case Snickers bar
that maybe one time saved my life.
And don't forget last year's electrodes,
stuck to my leg, the centuries of science
reviving one blue foot. Years from now
I'll be walking around on plastic legs
with a battery-powered heart and silicon eyes,
eating imported apricots and flash-frozen
chicken hormones. I'll think, again:
In an Ice Age cave I'd be dead.
In a Roman villa with household gods and servants
I'd be dead. In a Gothic wheatfield town,
even before the plague came I'd be dead.
As for how I'd make out if some terrorist explosion
disassembles the running water and highways
and burns the air, well, I guess
I'd place in the race to die. Last one left,
I figure, will be that weevil yesterday
that walked out the door of my microwave
right after I'd done the potatoes.

But here I am alive in a brand-new sweater,
using things, using things up. Mom asked,
those times I wouldn't eat my peas,
or sneaked away from the dishes to watch TV,
What makes *you* so special?
Meant, I suppose, to deny it,
I never did. And still say, I don't know.

Tyrannosaurus Sex

Did he make you scream?
In the middle of ripping shoulder meat
from a dead mound did you rock back weak on your haunches,
yellow eyes puddling cataract blue,
a pulse parting your messy lips?

No blinds drawn,
no struggle bulging over a narrow sofa,
no face-to-face reflection of cosmic bewilderment and glee;
he didn't gasp Faster Now God and no salt drops
fell from his armpit onto your breast.

Your arms too short
to reach anything, and the teasing air
open in every direction he might have gone.
Carrion no longer the sole desire
of your thickest muscles.

The moon so close
and the wild noise of insect millions
had nothing to do with your hunt through the cycad dark
to see if it was his teeth you needed
champing shut through your spine.

Musk Oxen Do Not Run Away

Got itself called a musk ox, never mind that half the year and
    more
its great Roman muzzle can only breathe ice and blow smoke.
Tell you another: These great stamping chunks of gristle and
    blubber
and hoarded hairy warmth are partial entirely to salad—
hearts of Arctic grass and willow tips. All ravenous winter
their round cow eyes strain over the ice for lichens and moss;
they chop their frozen vegetables from the snow
with hooves like patient gray plow-breaking stones.

Yes, they've come in for their share of guff
for those Fifties-hairdo horns. But they don't laugh much.
They're busy pumping all the blood it takes to live under half a
    sun.
When wolves come streaking in fire-tongues over the freeze,
they circle tight. Barricading the babies and mothers,
their bleating heart, and lowering like the sky, the old bulls and
    cows
kill wolves, kill wolves—with one bludgeoning pulse
strike out at last at an enemy they can see.

Neanderthal

Walking home from my powerless car
I pass through a dozen supper smells, each
more promising than anything I've ever cooked.
But then my neighbors long since left me behind.
They know just how to use sage and cumin.
They change their own spark plugs, prune shrubs, and feed roses.
In that garage a woman is caning a chair,
tight straw stars. My chin recedes,
my knuckles scrape the street I'm crossing.

My skills come from the wrong past.
I know how, in a team of two,
to bring down a marriage heavy with years,
cut out its tongue and liver, flay the skin,
break its mastodon limbs across,
and suck the bitter marrow;
you can last awhile like that.
I know how to forage.
I know how to sleep in the cold.

Lungfish Conquers Depression

Where the bladderwort and water lily
give way to bulrushes and pickerelweed,
and cattail heads nod hugely high,
every day for a thousand thousand
she keeps her eyes in the pond,
under the wind. Everything here
is as cool as everything else.
In the filtered visibility
she can set her chin in the muck
and submit her gills to the endless wet feed,
her skin to the close, slack hold all over.
No questions. Everything here is here.
Now and now and now.

She doesn't know
why this time she pushes past the surface tension
and wimples up the minute incline
on jellied stumps. She doesn't know
how far to the loblolly pines or what they are.
How heavy her body, wobbling on the peat
without support, in a shower of dry infrared.
So many edges. She feels a pocket
flex inside her neck, she gapes
at the scoured entry of demanding air.

Instead of Acceptance

I sank right down, it was a skill more needful,
    more evident than swimming,
I wrapped all my three-fingered claws
    around the rocks of the bottom.
No well-meaning dredge would get me,
    or the cold hands of delicate scuba divers.

At drowning I failed; it turned out I knew how
    to breathe under fathoms of pressure
that held my eyes closed, that worked in my fissures and
    washed some parts of me loose,
and the cold that would not kill me kept the rest
    from rotting away.

It took more time than death, but the whale I sank
    to be swallowed by I swallowed,
and surfaced, not your tombstone after all, not an island,
my gray hulk steaming, purple and green
    with disease that means
survival, and barnacle mouths in dazed Os all over my skin.

Dinosaur to Dragon

The predictable bell-curve brontosaurus,
dumb with tons and years, raises its head.
Extinction has come at last. No more swallowing rocks
to grind the endless meal of green needles.
No more subsiding to sleep, a carrion mountain,
under the bowed head of hunger on two legs.
No more need to love the Jurassic.
The little face lifted on the long brown throat
sags, it widens, grows lips and eyelids,
whiskers, fleshy spines, warts and spangles.
New bones, new colors open in its skin,
new toes flex and take hold.
New claws, oh it scratches the itch on its back at last
and the back sprouts feathers, the feathers have feathers,
the feathers on feathers grow feathers; gladly intricate
and hard to see as anything living,
its infinite edges intimate with air,
the dragon unfurls its wings peacock and tangerine,
leaves the ground ruby murex indigo,
lashes its fractal tail.

They Live Here

Bacteria live here where the river flows
acid and erratic, chocolate one hour,
navy beans the next. They form
little mats of excess, let go, float,
resume in a similar place the same
busy extraction of all they need,
mining or feeding. They don't take,
only change it. Absorb and split,
absorb and split. Making gas
too small to be bubbles,
not their concern. Not their concern
that there is no light here,
scarcely air, that all water is polluted.
And what matter if their continent
discovers alone an abandoned
North Dakota movie drive-in
and sits on the merry-go-round
for one whole hour crooning John Denver songs,
or heaps on a motel bed
before the Hitchcock television
with three music majors and a pre-med
and laughs to crying.
If generations hence it receives a glib final letter,
their wallow is slightly more bilious.
If generations hence at last it rests
an appendage on a desired knee,
they are swamped in unaccustomed
sweetness, which kills some,
encourages others. They don't strike back.
They need my life too.

Manatee in Honey

At first when the end of the heavy gold rope
filled and moved down my windpipe
I thought I might be supposed to choke,

but instead this too was breathing, only better,
and drinking, too, or eating—it didn't matter—
the heavy new surrounding that made me lighter,

the thick suspense whose pressure just matched mine,
that didn't dissolve, or muddy, or settle in sediment down
but rippled, caramel, on and on and on and on and on.

I thought I might die of foolishness at last,
being fed every time I opened my mouth, my lashes
held beautifully shut by pure molasses,

and a smile on all my lips that wouldn't go
because of a furtive belief that somehow
all this syrup for me was from me, too,

in spite of my own spite whispering I ought to
feel undeserving and moreover trap-caught, or
at least crave my old cold cabbage and thin salt water.

Honeysuckle

Helpless as an apricot in heavy sun
blushing into softness
or a sliced strawberry
drawing sugar into its flesh,

she turns on the couch to face east,
his house, she eats the limp scraps
of honeysuckle dropped on the chocolate box,
drifts over midnight wet grass

as if drowned by a single star—
feels a cool leaf edge, unmelting, draw her arm.
Puts all five fingers into a rose
and makes it open too.

Honey

Perhaps love means no more to the millennium
than saying, "I was there, it's true,
one bright drop fell from the mulberry onto the rose,"
or, "I saw this green branch bow and shake
when a squirrel chose it and no other,"

and perhaps the apparent favor of the universe
is no more than the crocodile grin of a Doberman
breathing hard and about to be hungry,
or the sun that makes a thousand prisms
wink in a blackened gull's petroleum coat,

but the racket and glow in this body, whose fluids
you have changed all to corn oil by kissing four times
the end of my thumb, knows otherwise,
and the very odds, billion to one, against great joy
confess its occasional visitation,

if not its relation to the clear brown band
around each of your tender pupils, or to
the note you just made in the margin of *Insect Life*.
To *Drosophila melanogaster* is vouchsafed honey.
To us, eternal verities, and this kiss.

Legend of the Woolly Mammoth

The eyes of these two fish imprinted in stone
look sad, small rusty sidelong blots
on traces of their bodies curved
like a question asked two times.
Theophrastus explained
that when the flood rose fish swam over the land
and laid their eggs, so once it subsided
their puzzled children
hatched in rock and were mineral.
They swam with difficulty,
whereas the giant red-haired Siberian mole,
big as two tents,
fairly flew underground, slicing
through permafrost as if through curd
with its terrible ivory weapons.
Only a blunder could stop it,
so the cold hunters said,
if it dug too far and erupted
like a mountain from the snow:
When it saw sunlight it died.
The trunk, the surprised splayed forefeet,
were eaten by wolves.

When I was eight reading dinosaur books
I didn't know any dead people outside pictures;
when I was nineteen I still hadn't met you,
thought I knew loss and didn't.
With you I learned to breathe stone,
to swallow Siberia.
Some days you played the intricate scales
that made your thin skin. Some days
you were only a silent roar
with impossible bright red hair.
But how you have changed me,
how you will always have changed me.

Don't you know better than anyone
how I still try to be your wife, your discoverer,
your frustrated music, your life, your violin?
—how I have to go sometimes
and stand on corners,
hold up my little slab of marked limestone,
my only surviving sketch
of you rotting in winter,
and say to passersby, You see, you see,
you must see why I loved him.

Where Thieves Break In and Steal

Tonight the backhand sweep of passing headlights
does not rake the front rooms too deeply
and the spot on the ceiling will not be a spider,
and though there is never nothing to be afraid of
the window is mended, the laundry has swallowed
the invisible broken glass from my heaped soft clothes.
Just now I do not need to walk through the house
touching, not quite trusting, the things we have left—
the turquoise heart, the gold pen, my grandad's viola—
or checking the clock, the doorknob, the eyes
of the stove, the bathroom taps
(the tarnished christening cup, the bone horse).
No one is walking where we have no attic.
No one will see the holes eaten in my suit
if I don't wear it. (The cedar box, the tin box inside,
the drawing inside of a face.) Meanwhile the sheets of our bed
lie on us so square and clean, we feel like guests.
But my hand is on your arm across my ribs.
We will get up in the morning. We can afford to hear
the traveling distant groan and crash
of night trains in their ungainly coupling
and the grassblade net of crickets just outside
where the little rags of petunias are ready
to be purple and white one more day.

Lassie's Left Eye

Lassie's left eye, rumor has it, was given to science;
the right one, at some charity auction,
went to a mystery bidder for thousands of dollars.
(Or maybe the other way around.)
So what was their last sight, the crocodile going for Timmy,
or the canine fleshpots of Hollywood?
Stupid questions pass the time
as he drives around Lincoln County for med school money,
harvesting eyes from people who died at home.
Like, is it true the retina keeps
a print of the last thing it saw?
The car picks up speed down bony old hills full of snakes,
four eyes jiggling behind him in the cooler,
and he wishes Bluebird Hamilton or Junior Sims
would pull him over, and have to look—
let their greater disgust wipe his away.
He left the faces closed and looking peaceful;
they don't have to wake to any more surprises.
Good thing only the corneas are transplanted,
what if a retina recipient blinked
and saw the heavy green flank of Mr. Fee's tractor
rolling onto his chest, or every time
he shut his eyes it was Mr. Story's nurse
pointing a spoonful of mush at his mouth like a dagger.
He drives the back road for a change, but outside Pearl
it's nothing but slow vines taking down houses,
and what if he skids off the curve beyond Coldwater—
he'd like to see Bluebird's and Junior's faces,
supposing they couldn't help but notice
the back walls of his two eyes and all four in the box
glowing with the robes of Jesus.

Accidentals

Mozart sighs and rubs his nose
and heaves his feet from bed.
He bends to glare at a blistered toe,
and eighth notes spill from his head.

Beset by chill and dustballs,
they fail to catch his ear.
They twitch the bedclothes' trailing edge:
Constanze does not hear.

Mistaken for bright beetles,
they are flattened by the maid,
who sweeps them to the gutter,
where they try to modulate;

then, sprouting into sixteenths,
they imitate black birds
that dot across the sky and sing
with neither end nor words—

but since they move in straight lines,
they stray out with the stars
and sound with other tuneless tones
beyond all staves and bars.

Chang and Eng View a Giraffe

Only the animal, from its laughingstock height,
looks at them without change of expression,
stuffed and a little dusty. They look back,
the joined Siamese boys, their connection bare
between their twin white shirts, their inside arms
crossed to each other's shoulders.
Chang thinks, If everyone looked that strange
we'd still be selling duck eggs. Eng:
If everyone looked like that but us,
they'd pay to see our short necks.
Behind them a lurking reporter scribbles,
"don't talk much to each other."
The giraffe holds its lumpy head high, as though
it might still spy acacias.
The brothers, wordless, turn as one to leave.

Back to the boardinghouse, back to the usual
evening compromises, when one wants to drink
and drink and fall to bed early, and one
craves a long night of cards and cigars.
In their room, beneath some stranger's tread,
they maneuver among their boots, umbrellas, canaries,
and retie their silk cravats. Shadows of specks
on the lamp's dirty chimney dapple their ligature.
They hurry on downstairs to order oysters.
All night behind locks the dry giraffe imagines
bending its goitrous knees, its mouth reaching water.

Really Big Shew

Probably God doesn't do it this way.
God's dinner-plate galaxies are nearly unbreakable
and twirl steadily, without the support
of any sticks we can see,
whereas this man in tails and brilliantine
bolts around the stage, sweating and grinning,
his zigzag attention in fifty places at once,
to twiddle this stick, that stick, and on to the next.
He nearly bumps, he never bumps his tables.
The audience loves it, almost as if
they love him, as long as he keeps moving
and all his white plates overhead,
boring unlikely holes in the air
like notes of music.
Long ago he almost died of tedium
in a desert river city, before he grasped
that a mind will balance more gracefully
on the unsatisfactory stick of a human body
if it spins.
Perhaps God, meanwhile, is more like Ed Sullivan,
poker-faced in the wings,
watching with a kind of wonder
things he knew would happen.

Borodin: Symphony in B Minor

Saturday Borodin answered the door
where Rimsky-Korsakov towered, blue specs on his forehead,
his arms full of tubas and oboes; they blundered in
through relatives, students, and cats,
    through the samovar steam,
the wide firm chords of Borodin's wife's piano;
    and they chewed on reeds
all weekend, twiddled keys and strained their lips
till Monday, when through the door went Borodin:
    Chemistry Professor
to acquire new exotic stains, to fascinate his classes
without a single explosion since the first,
whose little glass shark's teeth still sometimes
grow out of his arm; casually he might pluck one out
late at night while the B minor keeps proliferating,
new black formulas opening over the page—
a suspension of flutes in solution, precipitate cellos,
a sudden expanding solid of orchestra chorus,
later a French horn pure as oxygen—
under the small lamp, a cat between his feet.
Nothing ignoble about this precision, this resolve
to eat half the apple, to choose and aim
for Point C between dim A and extravagant B
for Berlioz, not so far away, raving with love,
staggering half dressed over the fields beyond Paris
ghastly with grief, one smitten howl mounting the next
and all for Harriet Smithson, while his friends—
Chopin coughing, Liszt now late for the night's assignation,
Mendelssohn smiling at the sky—attempt his rescue,
wander in circles one meteor might erase
past tall oaks pregnant with mistletoe,
past low pre-Impressionist mounds of hay.

II

❦

Circus Merk

Circus Merk, a figment, is named after the composer Joseph Merk (1795–1852), one of whose cello études sounded to me as I practiced like circus music. The elephants are named for virtues, queens, comforters, godmothers, and cleaning ladies.

Circus Merk at the End
of the Flandrian Interglacial

The audience thinned by the week; they came huddled
in cardigans, later down jackets, the puzzled kids
trying to bite into stiff clouds of cotton candy
or chew little bullets of corn that refused to pop.
At last there were only these few clusters
wrapped in sealskins trimmed with wolverine,
solemnly watching the blue-lipped clowns.

And the distant, ceaseless roar outside the tent
was not the generators, not the runaway lions, but
the glacier putting its steady white foot forward.

The band played its march, even more out of tune
than usual, raucously over and over,
the players' lips sealed to their horns,
till the palominos knelt and failed to rise,
the trapeze artists, ice-tipped, hung straight down,
and the human cannonball, curled in his cannon, slept.

Till the big top shattered, and jagged plates of it,
red white and blue, spun down over all three rings.
Now nothing moves but elephants, shifting
ancient foot to foot as melting snow
runs from their great hot necks,
and the twitching tip of the white Siberian tiger's tail,
and the slits in her golden eyes.

Circus Merk's Queen of Siberia

The Queen of Siberia mounts her stool.
Her stripes are straight lines in a curved universe,
her lips are crumpled night. She permits
the man in gold to show her his whip and chair
without incurring displeasure. Her paws
heavily cover his shoulders;
she lets him live.

Was she once a squeaking ball
of tiger-down with catcher's mitts for feet?
Was it her mother who sagged to ground,
veins rumbling with tranquilizers,
and let the documentary hunters
pillow her head with leaves to keep
her nostrils from the dust?

And perhaps it was her great-grandmother
who was tricked into a rajah's bullet
and a squirming death before all his mounted elephants
by a seemingly impenetrable white wall
that funneled her through the grass
with its throat-shaped U
made merely of bolts of cloth.

The Queen of Siberia
neither knows nor cares.
The only fresh meat is the future.
She tastes the air: This could be the night
the drunken tuba player, who fancies
the bars of her cage are a staff on its side,
carries out his threat to make his head E flat—
a gift to her boredom.

Twice, thrice she circles the ring
silently to shrill music,
then paces back to her couch
and red slabs of dinner.
Her every movement sheds the one before,
a swimmer ignoring the water,
sleek as a spear.

See Circus Merk's Own
Amazing Siamese Twins

Not from Siam, of course, but Cedar Rapids,
or so they sporadically claimed—sometimes it was Boise.
Even when Zina changed the story, Serena said nothing,
just sat on her half of their special chair
and counted cross-stitch, or knitted double sweaters,
and one year launched a tapestry
that covered their knees with unicorns and rabbits.

That was their compromise, when Zina
pined to run away and join the circus:
In the sideshow she smiled and waved, in pink and spangles,
and answered most questions that weren't about bathrooms;
Serena wore denim skirts and read a book.
Joined at the hip, they had to crane their necks
to look in each other's eyes, but rarely needed to.

So two weeks after Zina's three-ring wedding
to a stablehand, with Dido the elephant
as other maid of honor, and clowns in the cake,
Serena's elopement with the Russian contortionist
surprised even Madame Vashti's bowl of water.
The simultaneous pregnancy, however, it was first to foretell,
revealing the new design they would need for their chair.

Nine months later the trailer rocked
while Serena and Zina, taking turns,
screamed for a day and a night.
At last their husbands tiptoed, abashed,
into resounding quiet, to offer their scrubbed forefingers
for clutching, and found two tiny daughters
nursing back to back, joined at the hip.

Madame Vashti Sees the Future

With every year her widow's hump grows a little,
and though it isn't heavy like her fat scrapbooks,
it bends her to carry it.
"Are you really a widow?" the youngest child
of the Flying Nussbaums asks, just learning the word.
"Since the day I was born," she says.

Why tell a baby trapeze artist
you saw every one of your husbands leave you
in the shine of his loving eyes?
When you see foretelling pictures in water,
you have to learn to send questions away
with answers light as small coins in the palm.

She has come to trust the shallow brown bowl
that never shows her own future. She closes her eyes
when she leans to wash her face.
She knows not even to glance at ditchwater
that when she was little ran with pale faces
of women whipped from their villages, men chained together,
wagons on fire with the horses still in harness.

Five purple and red scarves over the shapeless brown dress
that engulfs her three-legged stool. Flustered circus-goers
offer the palms she won't read
and look sideways at her bowl, as if they're thirsty.
All her hundred wrinkles turn beautifully up
when it shows a boring fortune—
eating noodles, sneezing, changing the baby.

Other times diplomacy is called for:
Beware x. Don't count on y.
Not that she sends them to break their necks
stepping into the street to avoid black cats.
It knows how to find us, she says. Be strong.
Brace yourselves, it's coming.

Circus Merk and the
Spectacular Conflagration

Whether the lead chimp was smoking in bed again,
or one of the cables mistook itself for a python
and dropped a spark as it climbed, or the fire-eater burped,
we know about halfway through orphans' night
the first tongues of flame grew lizards
that made the horses dance on their hind legs
and sent the high-wire artists swarming their ladders.

And while clowns with blazing pants burst from the wings
past the poodles who, concealing their surprise,
jumped through hoops that were burning, the lizards grew
    dragons,
fed by the bellows, decrescendo,
of lions and elephants bolting down to the river
that flows by the meat-packers, past the corn sweeteners,
the cereal mill, dim in the lurid evening.

The dragons rimmed the tent with a hem like sunrise
that crept hissing up its warmed steel ribs
as a bright orange hoop, closed across the roof,
and consumed the topmost twisting flag as it fell.
And the children, inured to less lovely disasters, cheered
and stamped their feet till the ringmaster
doffed his hat, which collapsed to ash in his hand,
and promised it all again for the matinee.

The Acts of the Elephants

Sound of a mountain murmuring in its sleep
drew Timothy to his window in the pale part of the night
where he saw the humps of dawn-colored elephants pass,
saw the loose strides that took them down the street
quietly, almost in step, and the dream
he stood in went with them to the edge of town.
They bore it with everything else that makes them so heavy.

They were not exactly running away,
since every day they went back to the wagons,
but every night for two weeks they escaped
through town to green New Jersey, a wide place with trees.
Every night in the place where the ground was moist
Dido planted her foot in last night's footprint,
then Abishag did, Nadezhda, and Clemence.

They have to be large, with all they don't forget.
The claws that fit these scars, the iron cuff too small for this leg,
centuries of work and war, winters of crusted ice,
sweetness of yellow grass when the crust gave way.
The waltz and galop. They render it all
in pendulous vats of stomach and long, long guts.
In a week the widened footprint filled with water.

They stuffed their mouths with fiddlehead ferns
and wet striped maple leaves. They scratched every itch.
Eased out loaves of dung, flicked mud on their shoulders.
Tim may have seen them dance one Sunday in pink
    and green satin;
by now he's not sure. That year the lake was born.
His stepsons take him there to sail little boats
that start out bravely and don't know how to come back.

The Hartunians Form the Tower in the Dark

Grinning, the poodles bound from the ring
toward their liver treats, and once again the ringmaster
with his long arms and the loops of his voice
sweeps any scattered attention back to the center.
But Daniel, plucking at his tights in the wings,
can see that tiny pinch of apology
around the ringmaster's eyes.
Tigran is pacing. The lights are set to go out.

Tell them, Daniel's stare commands the top hat,
tell them how impossible this is.
Anyone can make a three-man tower
using their eyes for balance,
and anyone can cheat with a lousy blindfold.
It took my father, Tigran the Great, rock solid,
to make them let us perform it in pitch darkness.
"First time anywhere," the ringmaster chants.

As if this isn't hard enough,
Tigran isn't speaking to Tovma again
since Tovma said, after another fall,
that if he has to show off he'd rather
stick his hand in the tiger's mouth,
and he never wants to hear the word "perfect" again.
Now they run out on their toes together,
arms wide to show the muscles. Now, dark.

Perfect dark, which isn't easy either.
It makes the audience hold its breath, at first.
It hears—something. Strong men moving.
Hand to foot, foot to shoulder.
The father foundation setting himself in stone,
sons groping upward. Daniel trusting Tovma
because he has to. Ball of foot to hollow of shoulder,
steady, steady, the inner ear flaring huge—

People in the bleachers begin to notice they haven't moved,
and suddenly they want to. Just a hand from a knee,
two sweaty knees apart, a little popcorn sneaked to the mouth,
and someone whispers to someone that
    they haven't heard 'em fall, yet,
a little kid says how much longer, contagious rustles,
and boom, a spotlight hits the three-man tower
just before it sways, and Tigran scowls:
The instant anyone sees, it isn't perfect anymore.

Tornado Watch

In the gray-green evening, Per Breehagen,
The Human Cannonball, listens through thunder
for a sound like trains. That, he's been told,
is how a tornado sounds,
and circus people know trains. He lies back
in his hopelessly unsafe trailer. Per believes everything
they've told him about tornadoes, how one
lifted a sleeping baby and left it
unharmed in the crotch of a tree, how another
picked up a lake and dropped it in some other valley,
how they butcher cows, they ram straws or human hairs
through a barn door as if learning to sew.
He might shoot from his cannon and rise in a spiral
that never comes down, twisted tight
in the painted flames of his cape.

Tovma Hartunian listens, and loses count
of his biceps curls; slowly his elbows open.
He thinks of the center ring spinning like a roulette wheel,
the bleacher faces a blurred outer shell in the wind—
the way they look anyway when he takes his bow,
then a rippling ring of palominos,
a slower inner circle of elephants
stepping their grave minuet, and a spindle,
a still point at the center, the Hartunian
Acrobatic Tower. Or what if he
tames the tornado with whip and chair
so it dances before him alone, and curtsies.
Fearless, he offers an outstretched palm
full of—what do tornadoes
like most to eat? Everything?

For Dido, learning the elephant ballet,
baseball, and all the rest, the reward was oranges,
whose sharp taste still makes her uneasy.
So too does this early dusk;
she smells ferocity in the tightening air.
The Iowa sky is not tame yet—
she's heard it trumpet defiance before,
with a flourish of lightning tusks.
She waits to see if this time it will
reach down with its flexible trunk
to rip up the livid undersides of trees
or choose one peanut and go.

Elephant Waltz

Abishag, Dido, Clemence, and Nadezhda,
a circle, a square,
then two elephant pairs with a kissing of trunks,
and the music of two foolish tubas
galumphs through the ring,
a waltz with the pulse of an elephant's heart
to disguise their great silence.
Step left step right and sway, shift the great weight
upon the tough pads of their feet
and their high loose knees,
and the audience thinks they are waltzing.

But this is the dance of two hundred war elephants—
step left and turn—
as they wait for the armies of great Alexander
to ford the Hydaspes
with war cries half drowned by the rain,
wait for the pain and the panic,
their mahouts slip dead from their backs
and the javelins sting—circle right,
in a stench not of popcorn but blood
and the terrified horses, slide left
in the mud of the monsoon.
The river is rising.

And this is the dance
of a Bombay–Burma Trade Limited elephant—
softly step forward—
hauling a thirty-foot four-ton teak log
in between stubs of the forest and through the bamboo,
her wooden bell muttering under her chin,
along a wet precipice—back and step forward.

And if the log rolls she must whirl back and lower her head
so the harness will peel itself over her face
like the shrug of a girl's nylon slip,
and the teak will go over without her.
One more slow circle.
Abishag, Dido, Clemence, and Nadezhda
go to their knees, they lower their heads.
The audience thinks they are bowing.

Professor Enjō's Astounding Continuum Ray

Rhinos refuse to learn dance steps.
Ahadi, the young circus rhino, eats whole cantaloupes,
scuffs dust, tosses his mountain range of a head,
and sleeps. That's about all. To a trombone fanfare,
however, he enters the ring as promised
and runs in circles, five slow circles,
horns bobbing ahead of his bass-drum feet.

The audience itches somewhere it can't reach.
All those tickets sold for the noble rhinoceros
bursting through the circus poster like mystery
    through daylight.
Ahadi is beige, expressionless,
and smaller than anyone expected,
although with each pass his lumbering shadow
brushes the highest rows.

Perhaps this is the moment
for Professor Toshiyuki Enjō's Amazing Continuum Ray.
Bring out the elephants, north, south, east, west,
Ahadi the stolid center,
and if the professor switched it on, you'd see
how the ray is only straight for a moment
before it develops a fugue on the chaos theme

and laps through the ring till Enjō is up to his waist
in snakes, or smoke, with an interstellar smell,
and the ray is pure pink, but it's blue, and his explanation
has never satisfied the light crew, but never mind,
what about how it reveals that the ring's perfect circle
is oval, like a tortoiseshell, and mounded,
and covered with perfectly fitting Escher shields?

But the animals won't fall off,
bathed in the curling blue pink ray that proves
their mass is sufficient to distort space-time.
It weighs on their shoulders, it roils at their sides.
They remember when they were not the largest
lonely beasts on earth. The professor nods.
The tortoise remembers too.

Circus Merk, 25,000 B.C.

In firelight they move.
In the dark they might be moving.
Deep in the wounded side of the gorge
a black bear dances, a red bear stands on her head,
a dozen horses stretch their necks and run
around the cave walls, jump
the bar of a tiger's red belly.

Mouth full of black, the painter leans to the wall
and whispers onto the rock another black horse.
The animal says yes. At least,
its lines say I too desire this.
Behind him from a dependent outcropping
Dido the mammoth watches,
and the ringmaster, knees bent, wearing a buffalo head.

His horses need not run from his tigers,
his bears will not turn on him.
In the torch's gold circle,
drunk with manganese, he straightens
and outlines his hand on the stone.
At last he has learned a command besides
Die to feed me.

Toby the Sapient Pig

Madame Vashti's scrapbook remembers
Toby the Sapient Pig. The oldest volume,
the one with brown inflexible clippings,
handbills with deep lead-bitten letters,
flaking posters, red and black, that commanded
ticket buyers—except for pregnant women—
to see, to see for themselves

the five-legged calf, the toad born in solid rock,
the natural unicorn, the amphibious boy,
the lady who swallowed a needle that came out her foot,
Toby, who could remember which card you chose
or add any two numbers under one hundred,
and the babies that Madame Vashti's great-uncle
cleaned every Wednesday.

Her maternal great-grandmother's friend's friend's mistress's
washerwoman's sister, he told her,
lost three husbands: to war, then the sea, then fire.
She never had children, she just grew fatter and fatter
till her tired wits wandered away, and on the night
she forgot her husbands' names she was taken in labor,
eighty years old, and delivered three stone babies.

The engravings show everyone smiling harmlessly,
even the calf, their flesh paper-colored or red or black.
But Madame V knows the living exhibits looked pale,
a little gray, like the displays in jars of alcohol—
the two-headed snake, the snake with tiny feet,
the mouthless salamander—
and wary, as if a bigger jar might be waiting.

She turns a broken page. Toby died young.
The pig-faced lady replaced him: a she-bear, shaved,
prodded, probably underfed. The great-uncle
slipped her apples and showed her the other freaks.
When her keeper proposed addition and subtraction,
she put her gloves to her naked face
and shed real tears. She knew too much already.

The End of Circus Merk's
Elephant Baseball Act

Steen the keeper knew Dulcie's dung was wrong,
and the look in her eye, almost as soon
as the other elephants knew, and the way her knees gave
when she went down hurt him and went on hurting.
Shanghai Susie, next in line, mumbled and blew;
all of them down the row swayed and shook their heads.

The nearest animal doctor was young John Thorpe,
biology instructor at Bryson College,
who came with a diffident frown and hosed every mouth
with kaolin peptin—most of them spit it out—
and sat by Dulcie's rising and falling side
all afternoon, watching a humpbacked wasp overhead
and dreaming of fame and conclusive results.

Ever since the war his secret research
was designed to measure the presence and weight of souls—
negative weight, since a body is heavier
after the upward-striving soul has flown.
Insects, his instruments told him, do not have souls;
birds do, and up to forty percent of lizards.
The possum didn't. The rat data were confused.

Dulcie lies groaning, a mountain the color
of the dirt packed under them and its trampled weeds,
stirring the dust that wanders above her
and turns to gold in late sunbeams.
Steen, in the corner, asks his bottle,
How can the elephant baseball team compete without its
   pitcher?

Now her blood puddles in the left side of her heart.
Into a thickened silence
Shanghai Susie and Dido, Eva and Helen,
    Clemence and Nadezhda
raise their trunks in a trumpet call,
then twine them, two by two, and rock together.
Steen begins weeping, and Dr. Thorpe nearly joins him,
mourning the lack of any scale to weigh her—

besides, he can see her eye has released a store of knowledge,
and how to adjust his equation for that?
The wasp drifts in and out of failing gold,
sparing them the weight of a few drops of poison,
but not the interstellar dust that rains on us all
so we're heavier by nightfall without knowing why.

Dido Summons the Beetles

Out at Hawkeye Downs, where the big top sags and kneels
as cables are hauled in like anchors,
the ground is humming and the stone beneath the ground
as elephant calls to elephant
in tones so low they penetrate the cluttered turf,
tones whose subterranean corduroy waves
tickle the elephants' feet.

The Queen of Siberia, striping her private shadow, feels it too
through the fur of her slack white belly.
Reclined, she measures their meat again, for practice:
Dido, old and tough as wood.
Clemence, perhaps, whose left eye weeps continually,
or Nadezhda, who limps a little when no crowd is watching.
Abishag, the smallest, might be tender yet.

It's time. Dido, rumbling, summons the beetles, and they come,
crickling through the trampled grass,
tilting over popcorn topography. In the forest
they keep the space between trees,
which would otherwise fill with everyday leaves, droppings,
death and the discarded moments of tigers.
Here, they do what they can:

Shred empty wrappers, roll molar-shaped wads of gum
into perfect sun-balls, pink and blue,
smooth the rutted dust.
Dido surveys the fairground, and the forest it used to be,
filling with night. She rubs an itch from her hide
onto one of the four remaining oaks,
whose children are splitting sidewalks all over the county.

III

Capt. Robert Falcon Scott Returns to London

Antarctica calves, and calves again,
groaning like all trees that fall unheard.
It tips the worn, abandoned stations'
slush of boards and stuttering instruments
into the rusty southernmost sea of the world.
A few runt penguins poke blind heads
from the bobbing rime of ruddy algae
into the rush of wind through cloven places,
and under a gray-green sky, where upside down
the heat of his successors' stoves ascended
to the widening smokehole between the air and the stars,
Scott with Bowers and Wilson once more sets sail.

Such unaccustomed warmth is shed
on the cairn's impacted tooth in the broader snow,
the men in their flattened tent might almost wake.
Voyaging kept them alive once, if only so long.
He doesn't remember now how he wanted
(beyond prayer how he inadmissibly wanted)
to lead, to find, to be there first,
to name, to be namesake, to be remembered
by many many men who would never go.
Where the compass cast its perfect south shadow,
how much less wondrous the uncivilized expanse
with Norway's flag already battering the gale.

This time his dwindling vessel neglects discovery—
nudged from below by great reptilian snouts,
littered with small black monarchs blown off course,
stared down by a ship that rattles with broken long-bones
of contest winners, entrepreneurs, and widows,
whose marrow tasted of similar desires.

Past the equator—no one is measuring—Birdie slips away.
The ice floor cannot be trusted. Wilson goes, and the lamp.
Scott wallows on till the last inches fail beneath him:
His thawed lids open; he flies in his furs and leather
home, down the darkening waters to Westminster Abbey.
Home, to find the new creatures couched in its aisles.

Warming: Aletsch Glacier

In the cold world, some things were simpler,
like dying—everyone knew
you could find a place where snow took shelter
and lie quiet till the wind
brought you your voices.

And fewer of these black flies,
in a shorter season,
hung over us choosing skin to bite,
sipping from the animals' white eyes.
Now they rise in clouds from what grass there is.
They seek comfort, like anyone else.

The glaciers perish and leave high naked dirt,
abandon their valleys that fill instead
with ghosts we cannot walk on: the sleeping man
with his unstrung yew bow, the herds of small hairy cows,
the meltwater meadows.

Rivers of snow will be fairy tales to our children,
like the spruce and larch forests broad as kingdoms.
We lie in the slag and look high up
to the rubble line trailed by Aletsch's iron robes.
Three hundred feet above us our milk cows
used to cross on ice to their summer pasture.

Whether or Not a Giraffe Lies Down to Sleep

Canon Copernicus at Frombork in Warmia
picks his way among the rotting cows slain
by one side or the other. It was a small war
as wars go, or part of one too large to see.
Already time for a clergyman to clean
what's left as best he can; let a peasant woman
cry on his sleeve, let the merchants be
admonished back to market. He can't see the birds,
but hears their hundred voices from the trees
budding bare. Beyond them, soon, the stars.

The stars. Too often in these later years
they divide, and slide above his eyes,
but he has them, has their tracks in his books,
has them in their thirty-four beautiful spheres.
Always more work to do, of course.
And more work for Tycho, rubbing his silver nose
and its reflections of the world's best instruments
for marking skies, wondering why it still itches;
and Kepler, lusting over his ovoid numbers
unconsciously mended by two mistakes opposed;

and all the others, all of them not gone soldiering,
who grind their lenses to hunt for germs, who stain
their fingers among beakers and alembics, who stay up late
with moths, or brave a continent to find a camelopard.
Anything that lets them cover a blank place
with answerable questions: Where to find.
What to feed it. How to measure. What will be radiant
and for how long. They see a sparrow fall
and want to know how many birds per cat, how old it was,
its offspring, habits, parasites, and genes.

The damaged fields fill with dusk, with the liquor
that pools in the back of the brain when you lie down.
Canon Copernicus, nephew of Waczenrode,
will write one book on economy, one on the heavens
(which way the stars go, why the sun is the center),
will do geometry and do good.
No book on war, or why his brother died a leper,
why a turned blind beak lies just by his boot,
with a few wet feathers shaped by the absent breast
like the inner arch of clasped hands beginning to open.

Courthope on Pulau Run, 1620

Tree with the half-moon scar, cleft-headed tree,
tree with its arms out, tree with bent back.
Nat Courthope scrapes yellow mud from his boots,
thanking his intermittent God for this rain,
cursing Him (afterthought) for three years
on a Spice Island lump seven hundred miles from Makassar
with nothing but rain to drink. And for Dutch dogs
strutting their ships through the Bandas
to stop his provisions. One hour it takes—
without ducking back of the ramparts—to walk
this piece of dirt good for nothing but nutmeg trees.

Three years. The Company said hold Pulau Run
and gave him two ships. It was something to do.
Sea motion, equatorial skies empty enough
for chasing the circle that flirts with his vision,
ghost-perfect. Something to do for coin
away from London, where a man might be no one
to countless no ones stuffing the streets,
moiling on the bridge over the stinking Thames.
Instead: three years, no money, mosquitoes,
the *Swan* taken early, damn its contrary captain,
the *Defence* soon after—Throgmorton's men shackled
underground, with Dutch dung dropped on their heads.
Instead: watching Pulau Run's little green nutmeg fruits
swell, split open, and fall. Tree with bent back,
tree with its arms out, cleft-headed tree,
tree with the half-moon scar. An hour around.

"We have rubbed off the skinne alreadie," he writes,
"and if we rub any longer, we shall rub to the bone."
The rice is rationed. Two years and more
since Gunung Api, the nearest volcano, retched
and hot-shelled the Dutch forts as he cannot.
(To have now the ordnance shot off when first they landed.)
Waiting for mangoes to ripen, waiting for rain,
waiting for Dutch attack. "I wish it,
being not so much able to stand out as willing
to make them pay deare." He rows out
with twenty-one men, and a bullet
lets all the waiting out of his chest like a sigh.
He rolls overboard and starts swimming.

He evaded surrender. The corpse was recovered
and buried by Dutchmen, who proved,
when the mails finally came, to have been treaty-bound
to the English that last year and more.
To celebrate, they killed or deported the natives.
Something to do. Bowed tree, split tree,
scarred tree dangled the limelike inedible eggs
in which dark balls of nutmeg hardened
and webs of mace bloomed, acquiring value,
while Gunung Api still hissed and groaned
and boiled amethysts in her throat.

Of What Earth Has Eaten,
Something May Yet Be Found

The archaeologist digs shards of sleep from her eyes.
She pulls on shorts still crouching from the day before
and breakfasts with both hands. She dreams at night
of driving a juddering jackhammer down a mile and more,
or biting off hills one by one from a steam shovel's seat.
By day, of releasing some crucial tooth to the sun,
paintbrushing dust from the mountain range of a jaw
(oh, lucky horseshoe) and touching the place for its tongue.
She strokes the dirt with her palm for anything new to read,
for pieces of eloquent brain case nested like eggshell,
a lonely pelvis with wide expressive sockets.
As her sweat drops on her washrag's worth of powdered rock
she thinks she could tunnel with stubworn brush down
    to magma hell
if it were there, the baked clay and painted stone book
that says, "Here are the stories first told of the stars,
the liturgy of the tall gray circled stones,
the first words spoken, the first graves, the first fire.
This was the need for red and black hands marked
above charcoal beasts in darkness weighted down.
Here are the thoughts of apes that looked at the sky.
This is the face of Adam, who woke at night
and guessed that he was watched, and felt alone."

Near Combe d'Arc

goat with no mouth   bird without eyes
line, a horse back   horse, its head concealed
horse with shoulder muscle of swollen rock.
black pigment, dried spit.
here on the floor a dish to burn animal fat,
a mound of colored earth   another

crawl, slither, stagger, wade this bronchial maze
sobbing in its old air   your boots too flat
on floors rounded like palms of bare feet
through shapeless passages   seven stomachs of rooms
and see by raised flashlight the goat   the bird
blown onto the wall from his mouth and his and his

but they were not trying to tell us anything
nor are they now   all they knew they knew so well
they lived in the cave of it deeper than we can follow.
listen till your ears break and hear only
the cave's breath   all one intake exhale
or is it the blood in your temples

they never saw their own faces   only their hands
the voices in their heads did not speak our tongues
of neurosis and hurry   horse voice they could still hear
with the ink expelled from their lips   bison, panther
perhaps not yet so faint as to be holy
bear voice   bear fat's guttering light

they never saw the black-limbed animals
cease to move in an unwavering torch
like yours   low orange now, a dead sun, gone.
you have been thinking too long.   so guess
at their knowledge that the goat the bird
the horses are here in this entire dark.

A Lizard, a Stone

There were barren wives she made pregnant,
says Just Now, who remembers that year of no rain
and Auntie Martha—not her coming
but her being there,
her hut full of dry hanging bunches,
and No More's healed foot, the sick baby well,
everyone secretly knowing what else she could do.
Freedom's childless wife was first,
then Up And Down's, and Rectify's,
then Laugh At's, who had no sons,
and Better's, who was too old—
down drawing water, all the women laughing and swollen.

Ukai remembers her sister wide-eyed before dawn
saying This is no baby,
this is no baby I carry, promise don't tell,
I feel chameleon lizard fingers
open and close in there, and its tail unspool.
A few whispers later they knew Tinofa
carried a yam, like all those yams she'd been craving,
Chipo's belly sheltered a stone
or an empty bowl, and Tsitsi felt under her hands
the movements of a fish. The door
of Auntie Martha's hut opened on dust
trapped by young spiders.

No one knew how to deliver such things,
Just Now says, and the ninth month passed
but none of them wanted to hurry.
He remembers the great heat day after day
and how quiet smothered all the men's gossip,
how quietly the women worked harder than ever.
Ukai can still see them, shapes in the fields,
feet planted wide apart next to the short dry corn,
bending up from their hoes
with knuckles pressed to their backs at the waist—
where their waists used to be—
listening out through the lapis sky for thunder.

Slides from Patagonia, 1896–99

Slide 1.
Patagonia on the map.
It doesn't look big enough, does it,
to hide vast Pyrotherium deposits
for years from a man who dreams of them
as magnets dream of iron.
2.
The SS *Galileo* sets sail
from Brooklyn for the Argentine.
A few minutes later a fog came down
and forced her to anchor a day and a night.
5.
They landed at Port Desire, where
abandoned cherry trees leaned on Spanish ruins.
The cliffs of marbled red porphyry
looked rather like the elderly beef
slaughtered that day on the beach.
12.
Governor Mayer's estancia.
Even in winter, no fire indoors.
14.
The horses and wagon.
Hatcher and Peterson set forth.
17.
Hatcher's first two guanacos,
shot for the museum.
18.
The guanacos lacking eyes and tongues,
plucked, while Hatcher fetched his tape line,
by carrion hawks.

27.
Hatcher paces thirty-one steps in the sand,
end to end of a beached, half-buried whale
whose skeleton he longs to bear away.
If only his back were broad as a ship,
and the shipping free.
30.
Cape Fairweather beds.
From the Santa Cruzian epoch:
Boryhyaena, Theosodon,
Diadiaphorus, many others.
36.
Troglodytes hornensis,
the little brown wren.
40.
Hatcher wearing two handkerchiefs under his hat.
Struck by his horse with its broken bit, he left
a trail of blood on the grass from the Rio Chico
halfway to Ooshii Aike.
42.
Greenland. Greenland? That was only
in his delirium.
55.
Lava beds at Palli Aike.
67.
The stranded boat they found by the Santa Cruz River
and mended well enough for one crossing.
Inside were two dozen bottles of Worcestershire sauce.
71.
The badlands of Chalia, near Mount Observation.
72.
Abderites crassiramus,
shining little black teeth in a lovely jaw.

78.

Hatcher climbs a 3,000–foot bluff beside Mayer Basin.

79.

He gazes at a nearly perfect forelimb
in a pink stratum near the summit,
estimates the humerus alone at two hundred pounds,
and wants it, wants it, wants it.

80.

Gazes at it again as he leaves.

81–83.

Mimus patagonicus,
the Patagonian mocking bird.
Zenaida auriculata, a dove.
Asio accipitrinus, the short-eared owl.

95.

Here we see Hatcher walking on a beech forest.
For a mile or more,
its writhing reddish trunks
were too thick to penetrate.
He set his boots on their leafy necks and kept going.

101.

And as they make their way back toward Gallegos,
he looks at that forelimb again.

105.

Blackness. Sorry, is that a slide?
Must be that moonless night the horses bolted.

112.

Rio Chico again, made savory at the ford
with most of their supplies of sugar and salt.

136.

April, east of Lake Gio. Making camp,
Hatcher admits to rheumatism.
A plaster on each knee.

137.

Snow.

138–152.
Snow.
153.
Hatcher on crutches; midwinter.
159.
Final return to the nearest town on horseback.
Three years in the field, and not a single
Pyrotherium bone.
162.
Old monastery's museum at Entre Rios.
The attendant urges Hatcher away
from a shelf of fossils toward the carefully labeled jars
that hold the hearts of saints.
Hatcher nods politely, thinking, *Repulsive souvenirs.*
Unlike the dusty chunks of matrix,
probably Triassic, the hearts
are merely from recent people, like himself,
and not of much interest.

Arsinoitherium
(Fayum, 35 million years)

How beautiful the flanks of his beloved,
her long back like a river's edge,
her rounded limbs, as she bathes her feet in the Nile.
How she raises the crown of her horns, shining
with water that falls to her lips.

The breath of her slanting nostrils was sweet with leaves.
Taller than mastodons' was her golden shoulder.

Return, great trees of the forest, elder river,
where the desert closes salt hands on the Qarun lake!
Loosed from the high rock's side,
the horns of his beloved fall from Jebel Qatrani
tonight, and the wind eats her bones.

Solipsist in Love

For so many conscious years, how convenient it was.
A relief to know that with one shut door
he could switch off every mannequin at a nonexistent party.
With what largesse he might bring them back
to chattering ingratitude. Earlier still,
to snuff out stars by thousands with one raised hand
amused him, when some boring bedtime
required him to put away his parents.
But now she has sprung from the program of mild surprises,
demanding his constant attention;
he is dazed with maintaining her, but cannot bear
one handsome elbow's moment to be lost—
must circle her, reestablishing the lion curve of her back
at the cost of a breast's eclipse to be speedily remedied,
must affirm her previously unimagined lips, call forth again
the mole behind her knee, his dutiful hands
keeping her three dimensions. He lets her laugh,
tolerates her most fantastic statements;
he knows she has somehow guessed she is not like the stars—
obligingly there whenever he opened his fingers.

Venus of Judith River

Buried in this landscape's rocky mess,
shank and socket are fitted to dry cement
as long ago they fit their looming flesh.
The bone shapes of violence repressed
melt by Q-Tip flicks to the sunny surface.
We're ready, we crave terminable moments
of a gagging fear that in the past seemed endless.

Crawling with care that looks like reverence,
we bring back just enough. Of course
her arms are gone, which habit bent,
tipped with arrowheads, over the terrible breast
not yet exposed to age by slipping skin.
We pick her teeth, gloatingly rehearse
how large she was, how she could hurt us, then.

Positive White

After a while you assent. The bread and water
you the jailer admit through the unlocked bars
don't force you to taste them and sometimes
you have to swallow anyway. Each interval

is one more lick of whitewash on the wall
or the clock face or the window
or the potted plant in its tedious optimism
dragging out leaf on leaf too slowly to be caught

in the act, but never running down. Spit on it
and it thanks you. Most of the rest
is covered now, the radio's insect eye,
the impassioned graffiti's news and equations,

and an uncreased unflowered sheet
draped over the raucous parrots in your head
has startled them to silence—at last convinced
you will not feed them, will not pay attention.

After a while you no longer see the need
to turn the pages, twiddle your foot in the air,
push your chair from the table or stroke
the smooth stone in your pocket, or pick it up

when it falls. You'll grow used to the hissing audible
once the machinery stops. To the height from which
the galaxy is a film of milk
twirling on a glassful of dishwater.

Fossil Finds

Suppose they dug him up one day,
his poems long since lost, his letters
scraps of blackened batwing burned and flown
and crumbled with their crabbed ancient characters,
and only found his head, stone bowl
of brains, their curves and crenellations grayer stone
from seepage faithful to the faintest teasing thought.
And the first slice of a reverent diamond saw
exposed the tracings of the veins
of some small leafy kindness—
Praise be the past wrote something we can read, they'd say.
Much later they would find in his skull the fossil herds
of vast misshapen hungers with their stomachs full of ferns,
the angular winged things with claw-hammer heads
and nails for fingers,
the huge two-legged anger's wide jaws lined with knives,
its crooked, feeble arms.

His Hot Breath on Her Cheek

Delicately they select the wet mangrove tangle,
island where nothing is dry, and the barrier reef
they will study to save. One will dangle
on bubble umbilicus down the shocking blue cliff,

tearing gorgonian fans from the fractal wall:
See how it changes color, see how it closes.
Another bands plastic bags of dye over coral;
X rays later ask how it took its doses.

Another with coral blocks set between his knees
slowly hammers out their secret worms,
another irradiates blue-green and calcareous algaes
and tinily slices the great Greek brown sponge urns,

two more plot the extensive line of holes
for informative cores sucked out by submarine drills,
one anoints clams with relaxing chemicals
so they open, open to his eyes as if they willed.

The transparent amphipod with salt-spoon claws
drifts glistening across the tabled slide.
Gravely the microscope attends its nerves,
its delicate sac of red beneath black eyes.

Now, bent upon the tank where they re-create
all reef conditions, calculable and mutable,
a tender love-light ripples in their faces.
I understand you now. You beautiful.

El Abuelo

Spirits of the dead, I have come to your mountain jungle
to sap the walls of your fortresses, open your graves,
and tread on your rubbery bones.
Where vines covered with moss choke moss-covered vines
in a stench of rotten lilacs, I'll hack a way
to your most hidden lakes. I'll dredge up
the gold chain seven hundred feet long,
uncover the gold cups and salvers and basins,
gold bowls with wide jade eyes,
gold model potatoes, solid gold corn on the cob.
I come from far away, in machine-made boots,
I watch TV by an air conditioner there.
I'll cut down your big red flowers,
I'll drag your thin air through my city-black lungs.
I'll squeeze your skulls in either hand
and leave you nothing but stories.

All the men in the village chew coca leaves.
Green mouths and brackish eyes.
The grandfather, they say, *el abuelo,*
strikes gravediggers, strikes any men
who even enter the ancient circular houses.
You find them where they gave up crawling,
their fingers sunk in the dirt,
dead of all the diseases at once
that ever the ancient ones suffered.
The *antimonia*, they say, that comes
from breathing dust you stir up among those stones.
Then you cough up all the blood in your body.
And what about the *relámpago,* they say,
when you draw too close to the secret cities
and hear a clap of thunder before
the lightning runs you through.

Old ones! this is your disrespectful grandson,
the one who is soft, the one who forgot your gods,
who pins your black butterflies to cardboard,
come to steal whatever's left.
Look, I'm stamping in the dirt
that's filled your roofless walls to the brim.
So poke a hole in me and drain me dry,
rack me on a bed of snakes,
short out my wiring.
I don't hear anything coming.
You should be afraid, when only a few
green-drooling goatherds remember your powers.
Come and get me, grandfather,
be terrible.
Acknowledge me.
Say I'm here, I'm yours.

The Wreck of the *General Grant*

No one in this boardinghouse, none in the city,
knows what he knows. They pass the cabbage,
they pass him on the stairs; they don't ask,
swallowing, if it was two hundred pounds of gold
lost in the cavern waves, or nine tons
as rumored. Sometimes they speak of the weather,
or trains. The simple water
quakes in their glasses as the express goes by.

They don't know the sight of a fog bank at evening
turning to thousand-foot cliffs that suck at your ship,
the suddenness of a hail of rocks and rigging
storming the deck, or how a vessel groans,
trapped in a slippery sea cave. They don't know
how easy it can be to let go a mate's arm.
Or how after three days of rowing it feels to land
on a scrap of beach that clatters end to end
with skeletons of seals, flensed in the years
when there were enough seals to come for.
Fifteen of you, tripping over their ribs,
with nine tins of bully beef, some pork, and five matches.

The *General Grant* was ten days out of Melbourne
when she slid with every sail set but no saving wind
into the cliffs of the Aucklands,
into the cave at low tide,
and wedged her mainmast in its roof.
The tide turned.
The ship moaned like a whale as she rose
and the mast was forced through her boards.

He startles awake at the sound, again,
but it's only a freight train breaking in the yards,
or the cattle crammed inside, or two drunkards roaring.
Or the *Grafton, Bluejacket, Anjou,* or *Derry Castle,*
wrecking on the same cliffs an ocean away.
Or the boarder who snores on the other side of the wall,
sleepers who snore and cry in their sleep
down both sides of this street, a hundred streets,
a hundred cities. They don't know
it could be the smoke of locomotives, or animal bones, or
   noise,
but it isn't nine tons of gold, that slowly
gathers in darkness, rising under our floors.

Primate Behavior

What was she looking for, the woman two days from
   the end of a wasting death
who told her nursing daughter, "Shave my legs"?
   Or the hospital-ridden one
who, coming out of ether, could only keep saying she couldn't
   be comfortable
without her panties on.
                        If one of us slips on ice, he or she
checks first for an audience, second for broken bones.
   We are the apes
with mirrors inside our heads. We pick our noses,
   we fart and enjoy it,
but this is rarely mentioned. We make fun of outdated clothes.
We listen to music.
             In a thick place of mountain bamboo the
               gorilla mother
croons and cradles her young one in her arm.
   With her other large hand
she catches her own dung and eats it.
   A hum of insects and green wet rot.
The father beside her sleeps. Is it eight-thirty Monday?
His lower lip hangs on his chest.
                 Alone at her golden oak table
the young lady licks her finger, dots at the grains
   of spilled sugar,
and licks it again.
            Close to the Pole, where daytime stretches
            like taffy
and icebergs move in vast and moaning herds, a furry man
scrawls a few notes in Norwegian. He cannot carry a tune,

but he can make stew. He has thought of little else but stew
and warming his feet for weeks. Realizing
how dirty his face is, he tells himself:
I am here for no personal good, but to help make maps.
I am civilized. See, the word *Forward* is drawn on my heart.
And he throws some dried fish to the dogs.

Vegetables in Space

In between the launching of satellites, the sipping of orange
    drink,
and the wondering if their toenails were growing faster up
    there,
the men in their glorious repeated arc beyond rainbows
tended the garden peas. Round-faced Mendel the monk
could not have bent with more grave tenderness
over his smooth and angular seeds, his long and short stems,
and his beautiful, ever so slightly cooked tables of figures
than these unshaven pilots, left without steering to do,
over their small and tentative passengers.
Plants were company of a sort, something to do besides
    exercise,
and they had a secret: Would noble generations yet unborn,
hurtling toward Andromeda, eat fresh peas?

Enclosed in their state-of-the-science greenhouse mist,
some never sprouted at all. Some broke into tendrils
whose spirals wandered in their weakened wits
and then lay down. A few, and who knew why,
opened their dimpled fists into resolute stems,
translucent, with a sheen like babies' eyelids,
that found their way in weightlessness, or the gravity
exerted by the mass of a spheroid seed.
Nobody heard them say, We came so high
but we don't see the sun from here, there must be none,
or, There is no *up*, we can grow any way we please,
or, Which way? Which way? From the food toward the light.

First Song for the *Ba* of Ptah-hotep

I was packed with resin and laid on my back
  with my head to the East,
my elbows closed on their hinges
  and the wrists with their few bracelets crossed
to make a loose knot over my syrup-filled chest.

Then I had all time and sand,
  while my fingers quietly shrank down dark and tough
like monkey fingers, while,
  losing its habits of bread and beer and cursing, my mouth
fell in like torn linen over my finally painless teeth.

But stillness was lacking.
  I was lunging like spilled water backwards; headfirst
my body—become my own Sun Boat, Moon Boat,
  flying at speed to burst—
daily took aim at the Sun itself, and fell, and missed.

Past time and dryness, past desire for the wooden slaves,
  the painted meat and drink,
I was collected, fledged from the shriveling flesh
  like its petulant stink,
and rode free of the wheeling at last, like eyes on wings,

to begin by discovering that all endless Egypt
  was only one tawny shoulder
of a larger strange beast-god, a soft groaning lapis boulder
always about to wake, restless, turning over.

Buprestidae, Cantharidae

God must love his million billion beetles,
he gave them so much to do:
bore into coconut palms
or eat apple blossom buds from the inside out,
spin and spin and spin and spin
on dizzy skin of a pond, or dive, or fly,
or jump with a click! from flower to leaf,
or stridulate from caves of decay,
     Gyrinidae, Dermestidae,
     Silphidae, Elateridae,
or trouble the sacristan with a sound
deep in the wall, or glow in the night,
or cultivate a fungus to feed the children,
or roll and push and pat and prod
a lump of dung fussed into a ball
for burial, or infiltrate a beehive,
or secrete a sweetness for the pleasure of ants
that loyally bear them from place to place,
     Paussidae, Dytiscidae,
     Carabidae, Geotrupidae,
and so much to eat: slugs and snails,
wool and wood, carrion, pollen,
leather, fur, bacon, cheese,
honey, mushrooms, sagebrush, grain,
     Cupesidae, Lucanidae,
     Haliplidae, Cicindelidae,
till everything stirs with beetles
or their wormy young.
Leaves shift on the forest floor,
a teaspoonful of desert sand collapses,
fragrant dung mounds crepitate in the sun,
beams of cathedrals whisper.

Eggs wake in warehouses, pyramids,
the lips of puddles, bales of hay,
    Scolytidae, Chrysomelidae,
    Cleridae, Nitidulidae,
or eyeless animals covered with humus.
They never lack material.
Some of the million billion work at bubbles—
domes and blisters wrought of hardened froth
juggled between the forelegs
and attached to floating grass,
or of paste from powdered wood
in the seventh level of mazes through seasoned timber—
faithfully cupping a little air,
a little of what there was, for latter days.

Alfred Russel Wallace in Venezuela

Five hundred miles upriver from Santorem at Barra,
he left the Amazon for the Rio Negro
and then the Rio Uaupes, where with his dysentery
he fertilized the hideously fertile valley.
He ceased to believe what he hadn't known he believed,
that every blue butterfly is just like the others,
that no white-crested Brazilian pheasant differs from its brother
as he does from Herbert, dying of fever in Para.

But whatever unborn theory tickled his brain
the jungle droned uninterrupted;
undeniably earth devours the earthly.
Ribbons of ants poured from trees to mince the flesh
of his 160 species of fish,
mold deployed its furry mouths
on the butterflies tucked in his drying box,
maggots hatched hungry from monkeys hung out in the sun.
Kept alive, the monkeys ate the birds.

His own feet rotted around the burrow holes of chigoe fleas;
at night he made blood offerings to vampire bats and mosquitoes.
The boat crew drank his preservative sugarcane brandy.
When a man dies, his stomach acids begin
to digest him. (Herbert, my younger brother.)
One day a black jaguar crossed his path,
gouged him with its eyes, and kept on going.
Shaking his bed with malaria later,
over and over he saw the spots on its gliding pelt,
black on black. He could see them.

The fever ate him, too, for three slow weeks
on the *Helen,* going home.
But none of his bad dreams told him
he would watch from a leaky lifeboat
as her burning mainmast fell. Then four years' collecting—
his monkeys, parrots, parakeets, his toucan,
his rare and curious insects, every diary but one—
fed as he watched the never-ending feast.

Cheese Penguin

The world is large and full of ice;
it is hard to amaze. Its attention
may take the form of sea leopards.
That much any penguin knows
that staggers onto Cape Royds in the spring.
They bark, they bow one to another,
she swans forward, he walks on her back,
they get on with it. Later
he assumes his post, an egg between his ankles.

Explorers want to see everything, even
the faces of penguins whose eggs have been stolen
for science. At night they close the tent flaps
to fabricate sundown, hunch together
over penguin fried in butter, and write up their notes.
Mornings they clump over shit-stained rocks,
tuck eggs in their mittens, and shout.
Got one, got one. They shove back their balaclavas;
they feel warm all over.

The penguins scurry for something to mother,
anyone's egg will do, any egg
no matter how stiff and useless the contents,
even an egg-shaped stone to warm—
and one observer slips to a widow
a red tin that once held cheese.
Finally the wooden ship sails, full of salted penguin,
dozens of notebooks, embryos,
explorers who missed as little as possible. But:

The penguin cherished the red tin on her feet.
She knew what was meant to happen next
and she wanted it, with a pure desire
refined for thirty-five million years
in the dark eye of every progenitive cell.
And it happened. A red tin beak broke through
and a baby flopped into the rock nest, smelling of cheese—
but soon he was covered with guano, so that was all right.
Begging for krill from his aunts' throats just like the others.

Winter: blue ice, green ice, black sea,
hot breath of yellow-jawed killer whales.
Summer: pink slime on black rock,
skuas that aim for the eye. Krill, krill,
a shivering molt, krill, krill, a mate,
and so on. And though he craved dairy products
he never found any; though he was miraculous
no one came to say so. The world is large,
and without a fuss has absorbed stranger things than this.

Sarah Lindsay was born in Iowa in 1958; she received a bachelor's degree from St. Olaf College and a master of fine arts degree from the University of North Carolina at Greensboro. Her poems have appeared in *The Georgia Review, The New Republic, Prairie Schooner, The Paris Review, The Yale Review,* and other places. Unicorn Press published two chapbooks of her poems, *Bodies of Water* and *Insomniac's Lullaby.* She and her husband live in Greensboro, where she works as a copy editor and plays cello with the informal Quartet mit Schlag.